MANDALA COLORING BOOK

Color to Relax and Create.
Stress Relieving Designs Mandalas
And Many More

This book belongs to

_____

_____

A Few Words from the Artist

In making the artwork for this book, my goal was to create images that are not as challenging to color, but still result in impressive pages once they're finished. Basic coloring skills is all it takes to make these pages come to life, and my goal is to help you hone such skills through these images.

Your coloring skills will improve tremendously thanks to many different elements, such as:

Symmetry: The majority of the images here are bilaterally symmetrical, which means that each side is a reflection of the other side, thus creating a balanced and pleasing composition full of harmony. These kinds of images are very peaceful to color and they provide many opportunities to practice coloring skills in an effective way.

Mandala Elements: The images on this book also include elaborate embellishments made up of abstract patterns, decorative shapes, and elements that are constantly repeated. This will give you the freedom to play with colors so you can create unique patterns and schemes. I encourage you to try new color patterns with these Mandala elements so that you can find new favorite schemes and use them elsewhere.

Grayscale: While the images in this book are not realistic 3D gray scales, I still used grays for depth, dimension and lighting, and to make the images clearer. The grays indicate shadows and you can use them as guides for tones and to add dimensional shading. Please go through the Coloring Tips section if you want to figure out how to make the most of these gray scales.

Interesting Shapes: In these images, you'll find truly basic elements, but I've used them as interestingly as I could to create images that are complex and a joy to color. I also included many intricate, organic shapes that wrap around other simpler shapes to create truly interesting compositions. I find them incredibly enjoyable to color, and I hope you will too!

Engaging Characters: The characters in these images are magical beauties and they each have their own unique personality, look and mood. These characteristics are made clear and they come alive on the page. I hope these engaging characters inspire you to imagine how they should be colored and to add your own unique details. I hope they make you wonder... What kind of person is this? What powers do they have? What's their role in society? What's their story? All of these questions are 100% open for interpretation and I hope that you will be inspired to develop their character and make them real.

If you enjoy this book as much as I hope you will and you find it useful when it comes to developing your coloring skills further, I hope you'll take a few moments to review this book on Amazon's listing page. For self-publishers like myself, reviews make a huge difference and I also value everyone's feedback and support. I would like to hear from you, so don't hesitate to leave your opinion!

Sincerely Yours,

Emilie Summer